CW01175928

LUELLA AGNES OWEN

Going Where No Lady Had Gone Before

Billie Holladay Skelley

The Crossing Time Series—Book 1

Luella Agnes Owen: Going Where No Lady Had Gone Before
Copyright © Billie Holladay Skelley 2015
Goldminds Publishing, LLC. (2015) paperback edition (Amphorae Publishing)
Goldminds Publishing, LLC. (2017) hardcover edition (Amphorae Publishing)
Crossing Time Press (2023)

ISBN 13: 978-1-959489-00-9
Library of Congress Control Number: 2011928604

PUBLISHER'S NOTE
Without limiting the rights under the copyright reserved above, no part of this publication may be reproduced, stored in or introduced into a retrieval system, or transmitted, in any form or by any means (electronic, mechanical, photocopying, recording or otherwise), without the prior written permission of both the copyright owner and the above publisher of this book.

Printed in the United States of America

For

Allison

who brought so many things to life

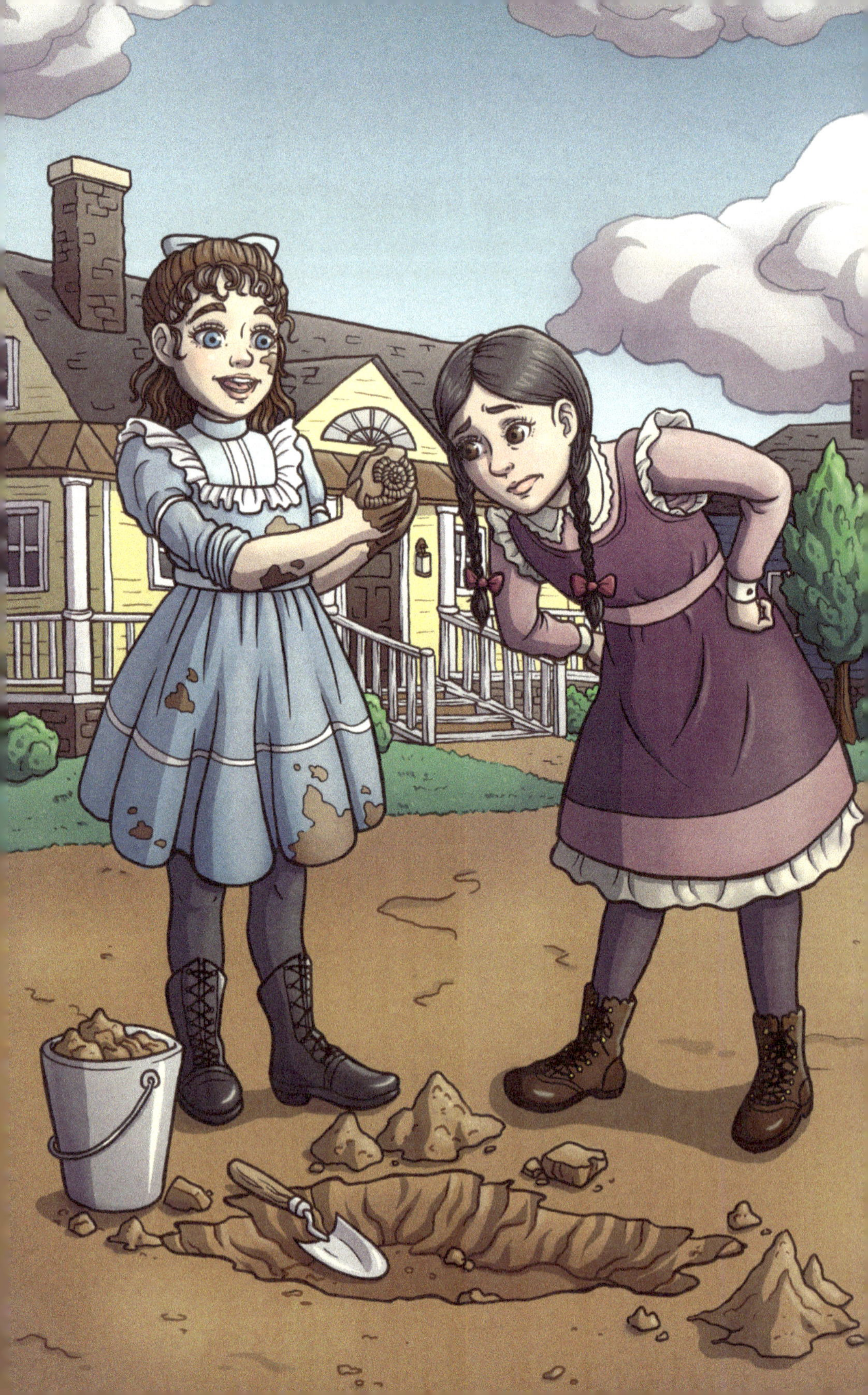

A Rocky Start

"Luella, you're getting your dress dirty! Your hair has mud in it, and you should see your face. Why are you always digging and playing in the dirt?"

Luella Agnes Owen looked up at her friend, but she didn't answer right away because she was thinking. She knew she wasn't playing, but providing an answer to her friend's question was difficult.

The street in front of her house in the **frontier** town of St. Joseph, Missouri recently had been graded and in the exposed clay bank she had found a whole new world. There were interesting rocks, amazing shells, and unusual **fossils**. How was it possible, she wondered, that these shell fragments and fossil specimens could be in her hometown—a place that was so far from the ocean?

Luella finally remembered her friend's question and answered, "I'm not playing. I'm studying the rocks and the shells." She held up her most recent discovery in her hand and stretched it toward her friend, "Look, see this unusual fossil."

Her friend glanced at the dirty rock in Luella's muddy hand, rolled her eyes in disbelief, and answered, "You know, you're going to get in trouble for getting your clothes and hair so dirty."

With that warning, her friend turned and walked away.

Luella didn't mind. She was used to her friends thinking she was a little different. She knew she couldn't explain it very well, but she was very curious about the world in which she lived. She wanted to understand it better.

For Luella, the study of soil, rocks, and shells was fascinating. She loved science—especially **geography** and **geology**—and it amazed her how the fossils, rocks, and layers of the soil could tell about the history of the planet Earth and the life that had once lived on it. She liked looking at land formations and imagining how they came to be the way they were. She enjoyed studying maps and thinking about the faraway countries they revealed. Best of all, she liked to imagine how the rivers, lakes, and mountains in these countries might actually appear in person. She told herself, "One day, I will visit those areas and see them for myself!"

Unfortunately for Luella, who was born in 1852, most young girls of her age did not study science and they did not travel alone hardly anywhere. Girls, at that time, were supposed to learn homemaking skills that might be useful in managing a household or caring for a family. They were expected to get married. If they did have a **career**, it usually meant becoming a schoolteacher. Above all, they were supposed to conduct themselves in public in a clean and proper manner—and that did not include getting your clothes and hair dirty digging in clay banks!

Luella knew her parents might be a little upset, but she also knew they liked for her to learn new things. They always supported and encouraged her studies. Besides, when you are studying something in the ground, it is impossible not to get a little dirty! She gathered up her new fossil specimens in the apron front of her ruffled **pinafore** to carry home. Once inside, she would focus on carefully recording and cataloging each one of them.

Luella knew that careful notes and recordkeeping were important in any scientific study, so she kept detailed records of all the specimens she found when she went exploring. She liked being outside—following winding creeks, climbing along the river bluffs, peering into caves, and searching for new discoveries. You see, Luella wanted to be a scientist when she grew up. There was just one big problem.

In the time period in which Luella lived, it was extremely unusual for a girl to choose a career as a scientist. She knew her family and friends would think it somewhat strange if she expressed her interest in a scientific career. Female scientists just were not the **norm** for Luella's time, so she kept her plans, for the time being, a secret.

Gaining Ground

"Luella, I don't understand what all the fuss is about. Why are you so excited?"

Luella held up the papers in her hand and waved them toward her friend. "You have to read this. It is the most exciting thing. Just think about it—**mastodon** remains in Missouri!"

"It's a bunch of bones in the dirt. It isn't going to change anything."

Astonished, Luella looked quizzically at her friend. "Don't you understand? In some ways, it changes everything. It tells us about our past and what life here was once like."

Luella's friend didn't understand her excitement, but by this time she was used to Luella's enthusiasm for unusual **artifacts** and strange news.

The year was 1869, and Luella had just read about mastodon remains being discovered near Sedalia, Missouri. Scientists from all around the country were coming to Missouri to study the remains and discuss their findings. Luella wanted to go, too.

She was now a teenager and a young lady, however, and she was expected at all times to conduct herself, wholeheartedly and absolutely, in a ladylike manner. For the moment, she had forgotten. The recent news of the mastodon discovery had aroused her scientific curiosity, and she was bubbling with energy, enthusiasm, and excitement. Her mind was swirling with images of how the remains might appear.

In a way, Luella felt the discovery was a sign—telling her to think carefully about her own future direction. Perhaps, it was a notice that she should act on her own career interests. Luella knew she had to decide where she was going to direct her energies in the future and what she was going to do with her life. Most of the girls her age already were married or were thinking about getting married. For Luella, however, the flame of a new scientific interest had been burning in the depths of her mind, and she couldn't put it out.

She had become fascinated with **speleology**—the exploration and study of caves! Luella had been interested in caves since she was a child, but what was an initial curiosity had grown to a professional calling. She had read all the books and articles she could find about caving, but she wasn't simply intellectually curious. She wanted to see caves herself and study them firsthand.

Missouri is often called "the cave state," and Luella knew some caverns were close enough to her home to permit her to visit them. As soon as she was able, she joined groups on tours of nearby caves. Walking through dark chambers for entertainment, however, was not what Luella had in mind. She wanted to thoroughly study caves and describe them in scientific detail. She wanted to visit new caverns and sections of caves that had not been explored yet by the public. She wanted to see what formations and structures lay beyond the tours. In short, she wanted more. Luella wanted to conduct her own studies, make her own observations, and record her own findings.

Unfortunately for Luella, at that time, speleology was not considered a woman's field. Caving was viewed as an unclean, unladylike pursuit. It just wasn't thought of as something a girl could or should do.

As her childhood adventures had shown, however, Luella was not afraid of defying the accepted rules and **conventions** of her time. Intellectually she wanted a challenge, and her independent spirit longed to explore new paths. Caving fulfilled both needs. She knew she was physically and mentally capable of undertaking this goal. Her adventurous spirit would guide her. Luella realized she could no longer keep her desire for a scientific career a secret. This was the path for her, and she was going to take it.

Breaking New Ground

"Luella, it's unthinkable. Aren't you afraid? You could get lost. You could slip and fall. You could **descend** into darkness and be lost forever."

Luella took note of her friend's truly worried expression, but she continued to thoughtfully consider her plans. She focused her gaze on the numerous rock specimens on the shelves in her room, and answered, "I will be careful and cautious, but I have to do what I believe is right for me."

By this time, Luella's parents and a few close friends knew she was interested in a scientific career. There was no denying it at this point. Once her parents accepted this fact, they tried to direct her focus toward **astronomy**. Astronomy was a scientific field, and if their daughter insisted on

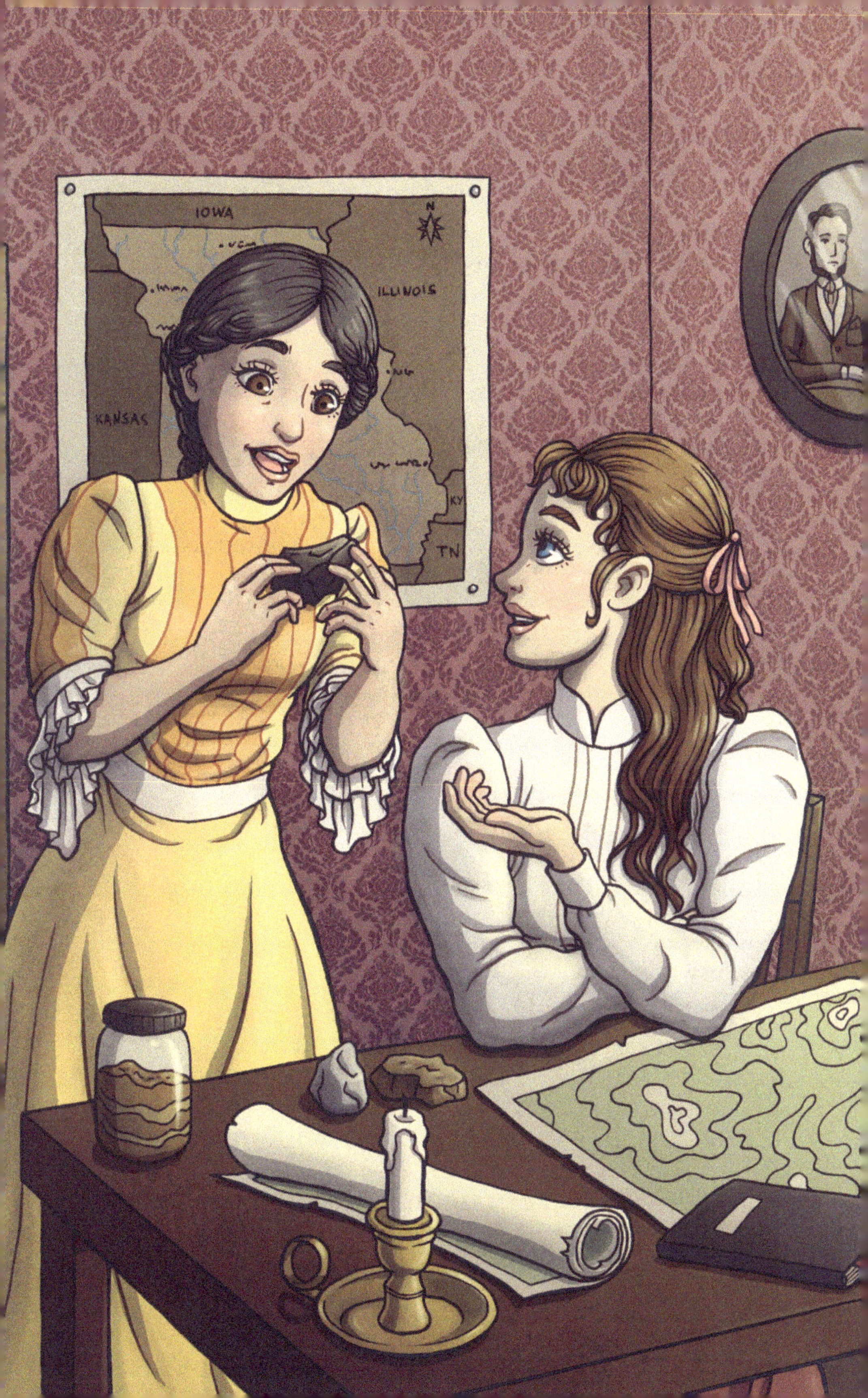
IOWA
ILLINOIS
KANSAS
KY
TN
N

science as a career, they felt astronomy seemed a more ladylike pursuit. They could imagine Luella politely giving talks about the stars to local schoolchildren and area social groups.

Luella, however, had always been interested in the study of Earth and its features. Her mind was made up. She was going to study geology and speleology. There were no female geologists or female speleologists at that time, but this fact did not deter Luella. She was making her plans to study caves.

Soon, despite the concerns of members of her family and the fears of her close friends, Luella was traveling by train, coach, and carriage to remote areas to reach caves she longed to explore and study. She often hired a wagon and driver to transport her across narrow, winding roads that at times were surrounded by rolling hills and at other times were covered by dark forests.

Travel at that time was very difficult because many of the caves Luella wanted to see were in distant, isolated locations that required many forms of **transportation**—including walking—to reach. Many caves were located in areas far beyond where good roads ended and where horse-drawn wagons could venture. Several were in isolated and remote areas where their entrances were almost completely hidden by natural **vegetation**. Luella would often have to find or hire a guide to locate an entry point. For some caves, entrance was only possible by crude, uneven steps, slippery slopes, or very steep **descents** using ropes and buckets. At these caves, there were no constructed cement

paths, no sturdy guardrails or helpful handrails, and no informational signs like we take for granted today when we visit a cave.

The caves Luella wanted to explore were often on private land, and she first had to write to their male owners to obtain permission to be on their property. Some owners were delighted to show her around and would happily guide her through their caves. Others feared for her welfare in such dangerous environments and refused. They would allow men to enter their caves, but they would make up excuses to prevent her from entering and conducting her research.

On one occasion, nervous men, who were worried for her safety, explained to her that the available rope was not strong enough or long enough to permit her to enter a cave. Luella was equally annoyed and frustrated because she really wanted to explore the cave, but she felt a sense of humor on such occasions was needed. She noted that cave rope often has an unusual and **peculiar** quality. The "peculiarity" was that a rope that could safely hold a two-hundred-pound man could suddenly and unexplainably weaken when threatened with the weight of a one-hundred-pound woman!

Such instances were indeed frustrating, but Luella **persevered**. She often faced **prejudice** and disbelief that a woman could mentally and physically undertake caving research, but she remained **undaunted**. Her determination was intense, and she usually succeeded in persuading individuals to assist in her caving studies.

By now, Luella was a refined lady. During her normal day in regular society, she carefully arranged her hair and appearance. She wore long, fancy, feminine gowns and was always careful to be prim and proper. In the wilderness of cave explorations, however, her regular clothing was not suitable. So Luella exchanged her fancy dresses for more practical clothing that would allow her to climb, crawl, and get extremely dirty. She found that an oil-silk hood and cape helped her to keep dry in damp cave environments. Very unladylike, but sturdy boots also proved safer on the slippery terrain than her normal dainty slippers and high-button shoes. For strenuous climbing and crawling, Luella also wore a shortened, divided skirt that allowed her more freedom of movement. Her family and friends may have thought she looked a terrible fright. They may even have considered her caving **attire** somewhat **scandalous**, but Luella was devoted to her research and would do whatever was necessary to accomplish her goals.

Luella knew there were many dangers and risks associated with caving, but she was both knowledgeable and courageous in her research. There were no electric lights or flashlights available to her at that time so she used candles and the white light of burning magnesium ribbon to aid her vision in the dark chambers. Following cave owners or guides, she crawled through tight underground passages, balanced on slippery edges, and made steep **ascents**. She carefully **traversed** narrow ledges and uneven floors sprinkled with sharp crystals. She encountered angry bats and dangerous snakes and often faced the serious danger of falling. She spent days squeezing through damp corridors and narrow tunnels. Her strenuous exertions often left her over-heated and breathless, but she faced all these difficulties and risks with courage.

For Luella, the difficulties and risks that she faced while exploring were a small price to pay for being able to satisfy her scientific curiosity and for being able to see scenes of great beauty. In her cave explorations, she found giant chambers, clear pools, and unusual formations that she considered breathtakingly beautiful. The absolute silence she experienced while caving was for her **awe-inspiring**, and the thrill of discovery, to her mind, outweighed any danger.

Luella spent several years studying caves all across southern Missouri and in the Black Hills of South Dakota. She kept careful and precise notes on all of her observations and findings during these challenging expeditions. She recorded each chamber, passage, and formation she viewed and documented her discoveries in detail. From these studies, she wrote several scientific papers about her findings, and in 1898, she produced a detailed book about her caving efforts that was entitled *Cave Regions of the Ozarks and Black Hills*. Her book would become a treasure. For over fifty years, it stood as the only scholarly reference regarding Missouri caves.

Luella not only explored and studied caves, but she also promoted **conservation** efforts to preserve them. She recognized that caves are valuable resources, and she felt they required protection from **vandals**. Over a century ago, in her book, she wrote that some of the caves she explored had already "been deprived of great quantities of their beautiful adornments by visitors." She wanted these natural resources to be preserved so their beauty could "always be honored and protected for the public good."

Luella is believed to have explored more caves than any other woman, and more than most men, of her time. In her book, she describes how a guide once told her, during one of her caving expeditions, that she "had been where no lady had ever gone before."

CAVE FORMATION

SURFACE

CAVE

RIVER

On Solid Ground

"Luella, you never cease to amaze me. If you're not studying or writing, you're traveling somewhere! And all the lectures you give, is there anyone you haven't talked to?"

Luella smiled at her friend as she packed her trunks for her upcoming trip. She was going to be traveling around the world as part of her professional work as a member of the American Geographical Society. It was 1900, and she would be gone nearly a year touring historical and geological points of interest. For Luella, it was an opportunity for an extended field trip so she packed her "field clothes" as well as her fancy dresses and travel clothes.

Beyond caving, Luella also wrote many papers concerning the history and **topography** of the Missouri River. She envisioned the river as an important waterway for freight travel. She also discovered that the unique yellow soil of the Missouri River bluffs was the same soil German scientists referred to as **loess**. It is found along the Rhine River in Germany and the Yellow River in China. On her trip, she was going to make special stops in Germany and in China to study and discuss this soil. She was very knowledgeable about loess deposition, and scientists around the globe sought her expertise in this area.

    Luella studied and explored throughout her entire life. She never married, but remained devoted to her career. She became one of the **foremost** authorities in the world on caves, the Missouri River, and loess soil. Over thirty years, through her book, articles, and papers read before scientific meetings, she gained the respect of her **peers**, achieved international **acclaim**, and **garnered** impressive honors. Her lifelong love of geography, geology, and speleology always intrigued and inspired her.

Even though female scientists were not the norm for her time, Luella became a Fellow in the American Association for the Advancement of Science and the American Geographical Society.

She was also listed in the *American Men of Science*. As a member of these and other scientific societies, she traveled all over the world sharing her scientific knowledge. She wrote papers and **corresponded** with other scientists until her death in 1932. Her **obituary** in the *St. Joseph News-Press* describes her as "St. Joseph's most noted scientist" and indicates that she was "the only woman geologist recognized by the Chinese government" and "the only woman member of the Societe de Speleologie, the French Society of Caves."

Just as she had hoped and planned, Luella became a scientist. She had to defy some of the norms and conventions of her time and sidestep some of the accepted rules for ladies, but she realized her dream. She was a **pioneer** in the fields of speleology, geology, and geography. She regarded these three fields not as separate sciences, but rather as three branches of a scientific **trinity**. Luella Agnes Owen devoted her life to this trinity. She truly went where no woman had gone before. Through her efforts, she established new paths for women and encouraged others to follow.

"The small eyeless fish had been noticeable in the water everywhere but now came swimming about the boat in an astonishing multitude, and as unconscious of any possible danger as bees in a flower garden. Having no eyes, they were naturally undisturbed by the light, so the candle could be held close to the water for a satisfactory examination of the happy creatures."

~ Luella Agnes Owen
Cave Regions of the Ozarks and Black Hills.
1898. (New York: Johnson Reprint Corporation, 1970), p. 100.

VOCABULARY

acclaim - praise and approval

artifacts - objects made by people in the past

ascents - acts of climbing up

astronomy - the study of objects in space, such as stars

attire - clothing, clothes

awe-inspiring - arousing or creating wonder and admiration

career - the occupation or job for which a person trains; a life's work

conservation - the care and protection of natural resources, such as water, soil, caves, forests, and wildlife

conventions - ways in which something is usually done; customary practices

corresponded - exchanged letters with someone

descend - go down

descents - acts of moving down or going down

foremost - leading, most notable, most important

fossils - the remains or impressions left by animals or plants that lived long ago

frontier - edge of a settled area

garnered - gathered, collected

geography - the study of the Earth's surface and physical features, such as mountains and rivers

geology - the study of the structure and history of the Earth, especially its rocks, soil, and minerals

loess - a fine-grained, yellowish-brown type of soil found in North America, Europe, and Asia

mastodon - a large, extinct, elephant-like mammal with shaggy hair and tusks

norm/norms - customary behavior, thing or things that are usual or normal

obituary - a notice of a death, especially as printed in a newspaper

peculiar - unusual, odd, or strange

peers - people who belong to the same group as someone else

persevered - kept going, especially to continue doing something even though it is hard

pinafore - an apron worn over a girl's dress

pioneer - a person who helps develop something new or who enters a new area of study

prejudice - liking or disliking one thing over another without good reasons

scandalous - something that causes outrage, shame, or embarrassment; disgraceful

speleology - the study and exploration of caves

topography - the surface features of a region or area

transportation - ways of traveling from one place to another place

traversed - traveled, traveled across

trinity - a group of three things

undaunted - unafraid to continue doing something even though problems are encountered

vandals - people who destroy or damage property on purpose

vegetation - plants, plant life

DID YOU KNOW?

- Missouri has over 5,000 caves. Kentucky, Tennessee, and Virginia also have many caves.

- A speleologist is a scientist who studies caves, while a spelunker is an enthusiastic cave explorer who often goes caving for sport.

- Some people use caves for growing mushrooms and for aging wine.

- Caves contain many forms of life, such as bats, salamanders, blind fish, crayfish, crickets, and beetles.

- Caves are very vulnerable to contamination. Pollutants in the ground above can harm the cave below.

- Twelve women from the Springfield Women's Athletic Club were among the first explorers of Knox Cave (Fantastic Caverns) near Springfield, Missouri.

- Ruth Hoppin, another early female cave explorer from Missouri, collected blind fish and other cave animal specimens. She shared her specimens with scientists at Harvard, and she has a crustacean named for her, *Asellus hoppinae*.

- Luella Agnes Owen became a Fellow in the American Geographical Society during the same session in which Admiral Robert E. Peary became an Honorary Member.

References Used to Tell the Story of Luella Agnes Owen

American Association for the Advancement of Science: Summarized Proceedings June 1929 to January 1934 – The Background and Origin of the Association and a Directory of Fellows and Other Members. Vols. LXXXII to LXXXVI. Washington, D. C.: American Association for the Advancement of Science, 1934.

Boder, Bartlett. "Great Floods." *Museum Graphic* (St. Joseph Museum) IV, no. 2 (1952): 6-8.

Boder, Bartlett. "The Three Owen Sisters...Famous Scientists." *Museum Graphic* (St. Joseph Museum) VIII, no. 2 (1956): 1-3.

Cattell, J. McKeen, and Jaques Cattell. eds. *American Men of Science*. New York: The Science Press, 1927.

Dains, Mary K., and Sue Sadler, eds. *Show Me Missouri Women: Selected Biographies*. Vol. 2. Kirksville, MO: The Thomas Jefferson University Press, 1993.

Eberle, Jean Fahey. *The Incredible Owen Girls*. St. Louis: Boar's Head Press, 1977.

Heritage of Buchanan County, Missouri. Dallas: National Share Graphics - Missouri River Heritage Association, 1984.

"Luella Owen Dead – Was Illustrious Citizen of St. Joseph." *The St. Joseph News-Press*, 1 June 1932, 7.

"Owen House Has Stayed Step Ahead of the World." *The St. Joseph News-Press*, 22 August 1937, 1.

Owen, Luella Agnes. *Cave Regions of the Ozarks and Black Hills*. 1898. New York: Johnson Reprint Corporation, 1970.

Owen, Luella Agnes. "Cave Regions of the Ozarks." *Missouri Speleology* 10 (1968): 22-86.

Owen, Luella Agnes. "Evidence on the Deposition of Loess." *The American Geologist* 35 (1905): 291-300.

Owen, Luella Agnes. "Later Studies on the Loess." (Oral Paper) American Association for the Advancement of Science. Kansas City. 28 December 1925.

Owen, Luella Agnes. "More Concerning the Lansing Skeleton." *The Bibliotheca Sacra* 73 (1903): 572-578.

Owen, Luella Agnes. "The Bluffs of the Missouri River." Internatl. Geog. Cong. Verhandlungen-Berlin. (1900): 686-690.

Owen, Luella Agnes. "The Loess at St. Joseph." (Abstract) *Science* 19 (1904): 533.

Owen, Luella Agnes. "The Loess at St. Joseph." *The American Geologist* 33 (1904): 223-228.

Owen, Luella Agnes. "The Missouri River and Its Future Importance to the Nations of Europe." (Oral Paper) Ninth Geographical Congress. Geneva. 31 July 1908.

Owen, Luella Agnes. "The Relation of Geological Activity to Conservation of Soil and the Waters of Flowing Streams." *Science* 37 (1913): 459.

Shoemaker, Floyd Calvin. *Missouri and Missourians: Land of Contrasts and People of Achievements*. Chicago: The Lewis Publishing Company, 1943.

Weaver, H. Dwight. *Missouri - The Cave State*. Jefferson City, MO: Discovery Enterprises, 1980.

Wilson, Suzanne. "The Lady was a Caver." *Missouri Conservationist* 54, no. 3 (1993): 4-8.

ADDITIONAL BOOKS YOU MAY ENJOY
by
Billie Holladay Skelley

Luella Agnes Owen: Going Where No Lady Had Gone Before
Crossing Time Series-Book 1

Ruth Law: The Queen of the Air
Crossing Time Series-Book 2

Hugh Armstrong Robinson: The Story of Flying Lucky 13
Crossing Time Series-Book 3

Hypatia: Ancient Alexandria's Female Scholar
Crossing Time Series-Book 4

Eagle the Legal Beagle

Ollie the Autism-Support Collie

Weaver the Diabetic-Alert Retriever

Spice Secret: A Cautionary Diary

Two Terrible Days in May: The Rader Farm Massacre

It's Almost Time to Celebrate St. Patrick's Day

Tapeti: The Moon's Keeper

Lightning Source UK Ltd.
Milton Keynes UK
UKHW020853250123
415891UK00001B/8